Then & Now
HARTLEPOOL

A fine view of the centre of West Hartlepool in 1964, before the building of Middleton Grange Shopping Centre and The Civic Centre. The building at the front on the right is the Armoury and existing landmarks include The Grand Hotel, Christ Church and Binns Department Store.

Front Cover: A scene on Seaton Carew beach during the First World War, showing a group of wounded soldiers with local volunteer nurses and helpers, on one of their organised outings.

ACKNOWLEDGMENTS

Grateful thanks are expressed to Mr Sid West, who kindly loaned two postcards, and to Mr John Cambridge who submitted five photographs, two of which were used, and to Diane Cole and Stuart West and others who kindly offered material which, unfortunately, was technically unsuitable for reproduction purposes.

Then & Now
HARTLEPOOL

COMPILED BY DOUGLAS R.P. FERRIDAY

TEMPUS

First published 2002

Tempus Publishing Limited
The Mill, Brimscombe Port,
Stroud, Gloucestershire, GL5 2QG

British Library Cataloguing in Publication Data.
A catalogue record for this book is available from the British Library.

ISBN 0 7524 2660 5

Typesetting and origination by Tempus Publishing Limited
Printed in Great Britain by Midway Colour Print, Wiltshire

A splendid group of fundraisers advertising, with the use of a decorated motor car, a 'Concert - Tomorrow Night'. Just what the concert was, where or when it was, is unknown but it would seem to be around the early 1900s. The location of the picture is Lynn Street outside the premises of Sage at No.6. The shop was probably the best known bookseller and stationer in the town, and continued in business into the 1960s.

CONTENTS

A photograph of a tram taken outside Christ Church in 1906, the tram service being run by Hartlepool Electric Tram Co. Mr H. Howes was the driver of this tram, and Mr Stan Cutling the conductor.

INTRODUCTION

In common with many other urban towns, Hartlepool has been subject to considerable change over the past thirty years, and more so within the past ten to fifteen years. In the early seventies someone said that the future of Hartlepool would be very different to that which prevailed at the time, and the town would be a place for leisure, a place to live in but not necessarily a place of work. Some of this is true today, especially regarding leisure, and it certainly is a good place to live, with many fine houses including Victorian, Edwardian and contemporary housing of very high standard. As for being a place of work, well, there is still thankfully a plentiful supply of employment opportunities although the type of work has changed. Gone are the days of dirty heavy industry when men and women had to work hard and long hours to survive and provide for their families. Gone are the days when workers were covered in grime every working day with little time off for rest and leisure, with one week holiday each year if it could be afforded. Employment today is for the most part clean, safe and involving conditions which would have seemed utopian even fifty years ago. There are high-tech business, offices, call centres, and small manufacturing industrial units. Leisure generated activities provide many of the jobs and opportunities, although there are some large multinationals in and around Hartlepool supplying steel, engineering, chemicals, motor components, confectionery, clothing, offshore oil industry modules, nuclear power, shipping, petrochemicals and others, often supplying to the national and international markets in considerable quantities.

Perhaps the greatest change in Hartlepool would be in the docklands area, where massive development has taken place over the past few years. What was an entirely commercial dock has now become a nationally acclaimed Marina, the home of numerous small and medium-sized boats, together with large residential areas of quality, shopping of all kinds, places to eat and drink from drive-ins to high class restaurants, although the main attraction has to be the national award-winning Historic Quay. It is a replica of an eighteenth-century sea port, complete with buildings and innovative exhibits all connected with the Napoleonic War period and now owned and operated by Hartlepool council, although it was originally conceived by the now defunct Teesside Development Corporation with assistance from government grants and massive private investment. Within the Quay is berthed the second oldest warship afloat, *HMS Trincomalee* (1817), fully restored in Hartlepool and a major tourist attraction. Next to the Quay is the Museum of Hartlepool, depicting the social and industrial origins of the town. Visitors from around the globe visit these two popular attractions. One section of the original docks continues today as a thriving and active port, so it would seem the town has the best of both worlds. Hartlepool today is an amalgam of the twin towns of Hartlepool and West Hartlepool, together with the villages of Seaton Carew, Stranton, Middleton, Hart, Elwick, Dalton Piercy, Greatham and Newton Bewley, and is so different from days of old.

In the 1900s local wits published quips and poems of various types about Hartlepool, including:

'On a clear day the visitor can, if sober, see as far as Redcar,'
'As the Entente Cordial is not recognised, French visitors to the Croft are urgently requested to conceal their identities,'
'A short stay in Hartlepool will make you stronger, especially in your language, Stay a week in Hartlepool and you will never stay anywhere else – R.I.P,'

'Far away from toil and trouble, let us with the happy throng mix,
Far from spring tides and 'Destructors', far from stacks of Clinker Bricks,
Where there's no 'Expanded Sea Walls', let us languish, quiet and cool.
In the lovely wooded precincts, of Health-fool Hartlepool.
Let us lie in Old St Hilda's, where the gravestones - laid in rows,
Mark the spots where past 'Resorters', and their frying pans repose,
To the Band Stand, where the noisy, ragged, urchins out of school,
Drown the music on the Promenade, at Health - fool Hartlepool.
Let us wander to the 'Croft' - where no bacon could be fried,
To the 'Spit' beside the Town Wall, where the martyred Monkey died,
But don't 'niff' the tainted ozone, of which Cleveland Street is full,
Or you won't survive your visit to Health-fool Hartlepool.'

In case an explanation may be needed, 'The Destructor' was a refuse disposal plant situated at Spion Kop and the 'martyred monkey' was the alleged hanging of a poor unfortunate shipwrecked monkey who was thought to be a French spy by the locals. The reference to 'frying the bacon' relates to a badly written document sent from London ordering that 'there be no more firing of the Beacons' which deciphered as 'No more frying bacon', which was promptly made law and all frying pans buried as a precaution.

To further clarify, Hartlepool is the ancient historical seaport, dating from the seventh century and granted a Royal Charter by King John in AD 1201. West Hartlepool was founded in 1847, to become a great centre of commerce and industry, the third largest port in the UK by the 1880s. Seaton Carew on the other hand has an earlier history, dating from AD 1135, and becoming a Quaker seaside resort in the early nineteenth century.

Shopping in Hartlepool illustrates an example of changing habits. Thirty years ago and beyond the Saturday afternoon ritual would be to start at, say, Binns Department Store, a shop noted for high quality, and from there across Church Square, perhaps calling at John F. Knights, high-class grocer. Then into Church Street and another popular departmental store, Blacketts, formerly Hill Carter, and past a number of specialist shops to the Athenaeum. Turning right into the town's main shopping street, Lynn Street, which included, amongst many other retailers, Marks and Spencer, Woolworths, Boots, Burton, and the indoor market with Bretts, 'The Toffee King'. There was the Empire Theatre and of course the largest shop in town, M. Robinson & Son, whose premises covered five separate sites; then turning into Musgrave Street, past or into Walker's the butchers, Charles Dickens' Tools, perhaps stopping for a welcome tea or coffee break in Piccadilly Ice Cream Bar. Then it is past the Pram Shop, St James church, yet another Robinsons, and along towards the imposing Co-operative Central Stores at the junction with Stockton Street, passing on the way two schools and numerous small shops, including Rosens drapers. Turning into Stockton Street past the Salvation Army Citadel, Kip Heron's Café, a number of public houses, John Pounder plumber and electrical supplies, Laddercraft, Masons Café and Cake Shop - and it is back to the starting point, Binns, no doubt exhausted and ready for the journey home either on foot, tram, bus or trolley bus, depending upon the financial viability after all that shopping. This shopping square was familiar to generations of Hartlepool people, and is often referred to by senior citizens as belonging to the 'good old days' - and who is to say they are not right? And one day will people of the future refer to the early 2000s in similar fashion?

A thriving Whitby Street, West
Hartlepool as it was around the
turn of the twentieth century; absolutely
traffic free and showing the General Post
Office on the left, which is now a night
spot and the Chicago Rock Café. Most
of the other buildings have been
demolished and as a consequence the
street has lost much of its character. The
public house next to the Post Office is
still there, although almost in isolation.

Chapter 1

WEST HARTLEPOOL -

WARD JACKSON'S

DREAM

Middleton Road, West Hartlepool Gas Works on 10 March 1911. The large queue is waiting to collect coke at 6d per bag to be carted away by whatever means were available, involving prams, pushchairs, carts and bikes. So desperate were the people to buy cheap coke that they stood for hours to receive the precious commodity. Nothing remains of the Gas Works or buildings, the town now being supplied with North Sea gas and, as the new picture shows, the site is now an under developed builders yard although there are moves to develop a DIY store on this land.

A view of West Hartlepool town centre in 1910, showing an obviously staged array of trams together with the manager, complete with badge of office, an umbrella. The photograph was taken from Clarence Road, looking along Stockton Street with Gray Peverell department store on the right with clock. The building on the extreme right is that of Fountain House, which in later years became a car park for the *Northern Daily Mail* and is now part of the *Hartlepool Mail* complex. On the left is the Public Central Library, next to which is the Police Station, both now offices of Hartlepool Borough Council. The current picture shows the old library buildings and the former Binns

department store, which is now Wilkinsons. The dual carriageway that now proceeds over what was formally part of the docks is a far cry from the tramways of old.

This unusual building of gothic influence has been used over the years for a multitude of purposes, including those of exhibition centre, dance venue, council chamber, theatre, 'Mayoress at home', elections, flower-shows, lectures, concerts - in fact it is everything a 'town hall' should be. The building, threatened with demolition in the 1970s, was saved by public opinion and outcry. The building on the left was the Technical Day College, which was demolished to make way for the main Police Station, which stands there today. The Town Hall is now known as the Town Hall Theatre, hosting plays, events and film shows.

West Hartlepool Town Hall was officially opened on the 30 September 1897 and built to a design chosen by open competition.

Howbeck House, part of the General Hospital, in 1946 was formally the Workhouse. In 1861 there was authorised accommodation for 209 inmates, in addition to fourteen in the vagrant wards. The *Inspector's Report* of 1867 stated, 'I believe the ventilation, light, water supply and general sanitary arrangements of the workhouse to be satisfactory. Single iron bedsteads, bedding and utensils are clean and in good condition'. Out of a population of some 40,000 in 1861 there were 771 paupers, and by 1920 the workhouse consisted of three separate buildings, and these formed part of the General Hospital complex that is now known as The University Hospital of Hartlepool, and is part of the NHS.

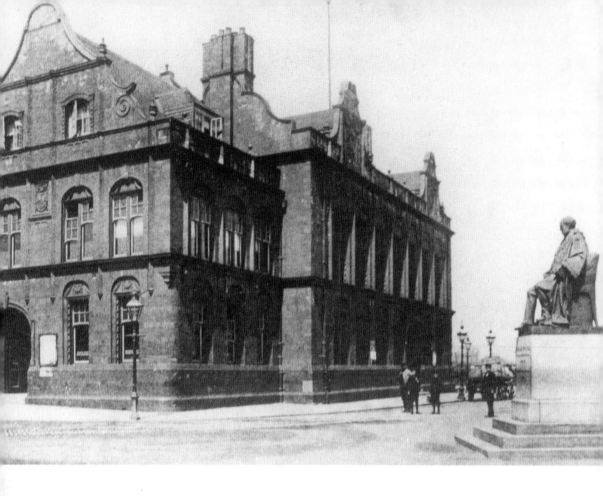

West Hartlepool Municipal Building, with the statue of Sir William Gray, Baronet, the first Mayor of West Hartlepool. The building, in Queen Anne style, was officially opened on the 1 May 1889 by His Royal Highness Prince Albert Victor, the first 'Royal' to perform an official opening in the town. The building's main use was to house the council offices together with the council chamber, Mayor's office and parlour. At one time the building was threatened with demolition, but was 'rescued' and completely refurbished in the 1970s at considerable expense, with finance provided from European Community grants. Today the building is used as offices by a number of companies and organisations, the council having transferred to new premises in Victoria Road.

Swainson Street before the building of the Middleton Grange Shopping Centre, the photograph being taken in 1964 and showing what had been neat garden houses, that would have been most unusual in a town centre, some boarded up prior to demolition. In the centre can be seen the offices of C.M. Yuill, Prolific Builders of Hartlepool, and who are still going strong in the town. Note the complete absence of yellow lines - bliss! The spire in the background is that of St John's church. Everything in the picture has now been demolished and has gone forever, replaced with the shopping centre.

Stockton Street. On the corner of Musgrave Street can be seen the Gardeners Arms public house, and nearby were a number of popular shops, including Kip Heron's Café, Pierce the Opticians, seen with the square-shaped clock, a fruit shop, a gent's outfitters and many more. The large establishment of John Pounder, Plumbers and Electrical Appliances, is on the left and in the distance can just be seen Binns department store. The photograph was taken in the 1960s and today the junction bears little resemblance to the past, it having been re-aligned together with a duel carriageway. On the right is the Hartlepool College of Further Education, which stands on the site of the original 'A' streets. Opposite is the rear of Middleton Grange Shopping Centre and car parks.

One of the busiest junctions in West Hartlepool was undoubtedly Stockton Street, Park Road and Musgrave Street, and on one corner stood the Co-operative Central Stores, while opposite was the Salvation Army Citadel across Park Road in

In the early days before buses and cars the most modern form of public transport, apart from the railway, was undoubtedly the humble tram, originally horse-drawn but as this photograph of 1890 shows they were by then all electric. This tram is seen at the Foggy Furze terminal near to the end of what is now Haswell Avenue. The cottages no longer exist, although the large houses behind the wall still survive, including Pineapple Cottage. This route, in common with all other tramways, is now serviced by local buses and is of course much busier.

A fine view of Church Street, taken from the tower of Christ Church in the 1960s and showing the extent of the street at that time. The empty space at the extreme right is where the church vicarage once stood and it is now occupied by the (empty) premises of Barclays Bank. The statue of Ralph Ward Jackson has been moved a little to the east to ease traffic flow in the area. Many of the other buildings remain today, Church Street being one of the few streets where little has changed architecturally, although the usage of the buildings has changed. The dock area can be seen over to the left and this has changed dramatically.

The Athenaeum in Church Street was erected and completed in 1851, having been funded by public subscription although 'Mr West Hartlepool' Ralph Ward Jackson contributed considerably through The Dock Company, where he was prominently connected. The building was extensively used for many purposes, not least that of The Board of Improvement Commissioners, a forerunner of the council. Used as a Magistrates Court and for a number of educational activities, including further education together with literary lectures, in fact the premises were used by just about everyone who needed a venue for social or educational purposes connected with the life of West Hartlepool. Today the Athenaeum continues to serve the town as a social and cultural centre.

This view of Upper Church Street at the junction with Stockton Street and Victoria Road shows the store of Binns Ltd (formally Gray Peverell) prominently in the centre, and was probably taken just prior to or just after the Second World War. Beyond Binns the War Memorial is just visible and this can be compared with the new photograph. To the left of the store the entire area was dedicated mainly to housing that was entirely demolished to make way for Middleton Grange Shopping Centre in the late 1960s. Upper Church Street together with Church Square is mostly pedestrianised, whereas previously buses and other traffic would circulate the area, as can be seen from the earlier photograph. A traffic control policeman can just be seen at the junction.

The Willows in Clarence Road was built in 1861 as the home of Mr George Pyman, prominent ship owner and Mayor of West Hartlepool in 1888, being the second Mayor after incorporation in 1887. The building later became the property of the Gray family and, as a thanksgiving gesture for the safe return of his son from the First World War, Sir William Gray presented the house to the town in 1919 and opened it to the public in 1920. It remained open as a popular museum until very recently, when the museum contents were transferred to the new premises of the Museum of Hartlepool near the Marina. The building now houses the museum services and archaeology staff and workshops. On the extreme left of the new photograph can be seen the controversial sculpture of 'The Watcher'.

with the well-known clock over the shop of Harry Lamb, clock-maker and jeweller. Being the primary shopping street in the town it was the home of many well-known retailers, including Marks and Spencer, Woolworths, Boots the chemist and M. Robinson. Lynn Street was one of the four sides of the 'shopping square' referred to in the introduction and so popular with Saturday afternoon shoppers, a habit which continued until the new shopping centre replaced the 'square' in the late 1960s. Little remains of Lynn Street today, in fact only one building exists, this being the Market Hotel, now an Indian restaurant. Even part of the actual road has been ripped apart, as may be seen from the new picture, which was taken from the same spot as the old one. Times! They certainly do change.

Lynn Street, West Hartlepool in its heyday, around the late 1800s. The street was named after Kings Lynn, it being also a port of note. This view is looking north towards Church Street and the large building on the right is that of the Market Hall, built in 1893,

V ictoria Road in 1966, looking towards The Grand Hotel and Binns store, with Victory Square on the right. This was before the introduction of yellow lines and parking restrictions. Behind the fence at the left of picture is the open area known by all as the 'Bull Field,' which for generations was used for exhibitions and celebrations to mark important events. This was usually accompanied with an Ox Roast, although during the Second World War the land was turned over as allotments in the 'Dig for Victory' campaign. During and following the war part of the land was used as a nursery for very young children while their parents were at work. The Bull Field site was

redeveloped in the 1970s and is now the Civic Centre and Magistrates Court, with the Hartlepool Police HQ adjoining.

On the 27 August 1940 enemy bombs fell on the town, including Church Street where the premises of Edgar Phillips received a direct hit, totally destroying the building. Also damaged were The Clarence Hotel and The Yorkshire Penny Bank, which due to severe structural damage had to be demolished, although it was 'business as usual' from temporary premises in Tower Street Baptist church schoolrooms. The exact time of the bomb hitting the buildings is recorded on the bank clock as '*ten minutes to one, a.m.*' After the war ended the bank was rebuilt, where it carries on business today, and the space where Edgar Phillips stood was used as a car park until relatively recently, and is now an apartment block.

The devastating effects of a direct hit on homes in Brenda Road, West Hartlepool. The raiders were obviously after the South Durham Iron and Steel Co. works nearby, but the bombs were a little off target on the 26 August 1940. During the air raids, of which there were forty-three sorties, there were seventy fatalities and 282 injured recorded in the Hartlepools. During the raids the local police force was constantly in attendance helping, together with the Fire Service, Civil Defence and First Aiders whenever there were people to be rescued, often while bombs were still falling. Great courage and fortitude were the orders of the day. All the houses were repaired or rebuilt and remain to this day.

Church Row in the village of Stranton in 1930 was situated directly to the west of Stranton All Saints church, and were the homes for people mainly working for the brewery of J.W. Cameron. Today all is gone, the brewery having taken over the land for development; it is now part of the brewery storage operations.

Victoria Road, West Hartlepool, in around 1910, depicting what would appear to be a Mayor's Sunday Parade, when the Mayor would have been either M.H. Horsley (1910) or Robert Martin (1911). The parade would commence at the Municipal Buildings in Church Square, proceeding possibly to St Paul's church in Grange Road for a service, but whatever the occasion the crowds certainly turned out in great force. The building on the right is the draper's shop of Gray Peverell, which together with the row of houses later became Binns Department Store and is now Wilkinsons. The original old building

and roofline can be picked out on the left of the new picture, as can the wall of the Grand Hotel from where both photographs were taken.

The Promenade, West Hartlepool, now known as Coronation Drive, twixt Seaton Carew and West Hartlepool, showing just how popular the practice of 'promenading' and paddling was in 1920 when this postcard was produced. The shelter would be much appreciated when there was a chilly sea breeze around. In the background Hartlepool Headland can just be made out, which in those days would be known simply as Hartlepool or East Hartlepool. Massive sea defences have proved to be necessary in recent years and a new single high level wall is evident to help keep the ever-encroaching angry sea at bay. The new Hartlepool Marina complex can be seen on the horizon.

Cameron Hospital, West Hartlepool, was built at a cost of over £20,000 and was opened on the 29 April 1905 by Sir Christopher Furness MP, the funding being provided by the Cameron family as a lasting memorial to Colonel J.W. Cameron, who died in 1896. In later years the building became Hartlepool Maternity Hospital and unfortunately this fine building became redundant and was demolished to make way for executive housing.

Grange Road, West Hartlepool, as it would have appeared at the turn of the twentieth century. The Electric Tramway service was started in 1887 and ran along this route from Church Street up to the Ward Jackson Park gates, which at that time was virtually in the countryside, the distance being one mile from Church Street to the park. Little has changed overall, the tram having been replaced by an infrequent bus service and the inevitable motor car as a means of travel. The tower of St Paul's church can clearly be seen in the distance on both pictures. Street lighting has greatly improved today in comparison to the tiny gaslights in the older photograph, and of course there are now yellow lines to contend with.

On the 9 November 1927 the official opening of the Brenda Road Extension was performed by the then Mayor of West Hartlepool, Alderman Arthur Hyde JP, and was accompanied by Councillor Wainwright, councillors and other civic dignitaries, and watched by members of the public. The road was constructed at an estimated cost of £70,000 - a considerable sum of money even in 1927. The two gable-end houses in Stockton Road on the left of picture were just two years old at the time and still exist today, as does St Aidan's church, which can be seen on the right in the distance.

Judging by the enormous crowd this is obviously a very important event in the town and could be the Royal Visit by His Royal Highness the Prince of Wales on the 3 July 1930, on his way to the Municipal Buildings for a presentation ceremony and reception. The large building on the left is the side and rear of the Grand Hotel, at the centre is the old police station behind which is the tower of Christ Church. The advertisement on the gable end of the other building reads, ' Watt's his name, for smart shoes'. Where the row of trees stand in the old picture is where Hartlepool Civic Centre now stands and what was formally the 'Bull Field'. The new photograph depicts the same scene today but also includes the War Memorial in Victory Square, together with the recent additions of four obelisks with the added names of those who have died for their country since the First World War, including very many from the Second World War.

Upper Church Street, West Hartlepool, in 1950 with the Registrars Office on the left, next to which is the Municipal Buildings, the offices of Hartlepool County Borough Council. Christ Church stands majestically in the centre, and on the right is a row of small individual shops, which included Pattison's fish merchant, Feather's Jewellers who are still there today, a gent's outfitters, Smiths Insurance, an optician and various others. Today the street is closed to through traffic, having restricted parking. The Municipal Buildings are now used as private offices and businesses and Christ Church is the town art gallery.

Stranton Green as it would appear in the 1890s, with its picturesque, if somewhat damp, cottages. The outer wall of All Saints church may be seen on the right, and is still there protecting the graveyard of the church. In later years one of the cottages was converted into the local branch post office and other retail shops followed prior to demolition of the entire row. The same view today is somewhat different and shows the modern replacement of what seemed then an idyllic environment.

A view looking east along Church Street around the turn of the twentieth century and clearly showing the early trams and horse-drawn carriages. Church Street contained many individual shops, the large building on the right being that of the department store and drapers of Hill Carter, later to become Blacketts, on the corner of Whitby Street. Opposite on the left is the Commercial Hotel which, together with Birks Café, provided a very popular meeting place for the ladies out shopping as well as offering reception rooms for weddings and other gatherings; there was also a shop and in the basement was the gentlemen's billiard saloon. This very popular establishment stood on the corner that leads to Hartlepool railway station. Some of these buildings survive today, with the exception of Birks. The large department store is now a hotel, restaurant and bar called, appropriately, - Hill Carter!

West Hartlepool Armoury stood where Middleton Grange Shopping Centre stands today, and was the home base for the local artillery unit, the 4th Durham Artillery Volunteers and Corps, commanded in 1885 by Lt Col. J.W. Cameron of Greenbank West Hartlepool, of J.W. Cameron Brewery fame. During the Second World War the Home Guard would use the premises for training and headquarters. The picture was taken in the 1930s and shows the grassed area in front of the Armoury, which was part of the Memorial Gardens, situated next to Victory Square. Today a completely reconstructed Victory Square is evident but nothing else remains.

York Road in West Hartlepool as it was in the early 1900s had many shops on both sides of this important shopping thoroughfare, being second only to the Lynn Street/Church Street shopping area. The tower of St George's Congregational church, which was erected in 1902, is very prominent in the centre, and the premises on the left are those of Hope's Auction Rooms. Many of the buildings remain today and York Road continues to be an important shopping and commercial area which now has a number of banks, solicitors and building societies, although the large square office building of Titan House does little to enhance this well-patronised street.

Church Street looking west and as it was in 1910, showing a tram and the ornate lamp standards and overhead electric cable runs used for powering the trams. On the left is the Athenaeum with Christ Church in the distance and on the right is the splendid building of The Yorkshire Penny Bank, which sprang to prominence for its schoolchildren's accounts - usually a silver sixpence per week if times were good, a threepenny bit if times were difficult, or, at worst, nothing. The Athenaeum remains today, as does Christ Church, and the 'new' building on the right is still the Yorkshire Bank, the old bank building having been destroyed by enemy action during the Second World War.

A steam generated fire engine mounted on a rail wagon, patrolling the timber yards in case there is an outbreak of fire. Fire was the greatest hazard at these yards and it is wondered whether the inevitable sparks from the engine actually started more fires than extinguished them. The Timber Yards were the repository for all kinds of timber, which was off-loaded in the nearby docks from vessels travelling mainly from Scandinavia, with largely pit props. They were ultimately destined for the Durham coal mines, where they were used at the coalface to prop up and reinforce the sides and roofs of the working areas.

Chapter 2

DOCKLAND

ACTIVITIES

The Hartlepool Fish Quay probably in the 1920s, when fishing was the most important and established industry at the port, with fishing vessels from far and wide visiting the home fleet port. During the herring season, Scottish boats would visit to sell their catches and there were so many boats, some also hailing from Holland, that it was possible to walk across Victoria Dock from boat to boat without touching dry land. The herring season also brought to the quay Scottish fish wives to augment the locals, who together would gut and often pickle the fish for markets around the world, and fishmongers in the region would advertise 'Hartlepool Fish' as a sign of freshness and quality. Today the Fish Quay is still the base for local fishing boats and visitors but is now operated on a much smaller scale due largely to the European Quota, which restricts the amount and type of fish to be caught.

W est Hartlepool Coal Dock in 1961, showing the Dock Master's office in the centre with the tower, and which is now a restaurant. The array of cranes belong to the William Gray Shipyard, the larger crane being a well-known landmark for many years and situated in the Central Marine Engine Works. The complex timber structure on the right is one of the port's coal staithes, where loaded coal wagons would be transported by rail along the top level of the structure, and the undersides of the wagons opened for the coal to be sent by chute to the holds of waiting colliers. They would take the coal to help fire London's fuel-hungry power stations. This photograph shows a group of local College of Art students on a day-out drawing exercise. All is now vanished with the exception of the Dock Masters office building, all the new buildings being apartments and eating places and the dock itself utilised as part of a fine Marina.

Union Dock, which consisted of 'A', 'B' and 'C' jetties, handling all kinds of cargoes from around the world, including iron ore for the local iron and steel works, pit props for the coal industry, paper pulp for printing, and much more. In the background on the left can be seen the internationally known engine works of Thomas Richardson, who was incidentally re-elected as member of Parliament for the Hartlepools in 1880, the same year Union Dock was opened. Cargoes from and to Union Dock were almost exclusively by rail, as can be seen in the photograph, which probably dates from the 1930s. 'A' jetty is still in situ today but as the new picture indicates is a very different vista with its call centres and offices dominating the skyline, the whole forming part of a thriving Hartlepool Marina. Navigation Point is in the distance with its housing, apartments, shops and restaurants.

Hartlepool, West Hartlepool and Middleton were the homes of a number of internationally known ship-builders of renown and prestige, but perhaps the most famous and successful was that of William Gray & Co. Ltd, who had a number of ship-building yards in and around Middleton, starting in 1871 with an amalgamation of a number of independent yards. Mr William Gray became the first Mayor of West Hartlepool after incorporation in 1887, and was later to become Sir William Gray, Baronet, in 1890. Local historian Robert Martin wrote of him, 'He was a plain, unassuming, approachable man of high motives and upright character, full of energy and with a high reputation unsullied by calumny'. The photograph, taken in 1966, is that of the main offices

of William Gray at Swainson Dock. Nothing remains of the offices or the dock, it having been filled in, now forming part of the Marina and museum area.

West Hartlepool and builder of the docks. The No.4 Warehouse is to the right of Swainson Dock and was occupied from 1933 by the North of England Match Company Ltd, who produced a number of well-known brands, including Memco. By the time the factory was completely destroyed by a disastrous fire on the 30 August 1954, the company was producing fifty million matches per week. The shipyards of William Gray can be seen at the left of centre. Where Swainson Dock was there is now a bingo hall and nearby is the Museum of Hartlepool and the Historic Quay, which at the present time is the home berth for *HMS Trincomalee*, 1817. She is the oldest warship afloat in the UK, and the second oldest in the world, and was fully restored to her former glory in Hartlepool by local craftsmen.

West Hartlepool Docks in 1950, with Swainson Dock in the foreground and the adjacent Coal and Jackson Dock. Swainson Dock was named after Suzannah Swainson, the wife of Ralph Ward Jackson, founder of

Sandwellgate at the turn of the twentieth century was a popular vantage point, for splendid views across the bay and observing fishermen and visitors on the Fish Sands below. Through the gate is Sandwell Chare, the home of numerous families of the Croft and subject to frequent flooding at high spring tides. Apart from holiday periods and very fine weather the crowds no longer flock to the Gate or to the Fish Sands, but there are those who find the sands very restful, and it can be the perfect sun trap – pass the sun tan lotion!

Chapter 3
HARTLEPOOL
THE ORIGINS

A fine view of the High Street, Hartlepool, c. 1910, which was a popular and busy venue for markets and fairs. The shopping area is now part of the Croft Gardens, the Croft itself having been demolished in the 1930s due to 'insanitary conditions'. St Hilda's church stands proud above the houses and on the right can just be seen the seaside residence of the Duke of Cleveland, who no doubt indulged in the healthy properties of the waters. The town was not known throughout the region as 'Healthful Hartlepool' for nothing! The Duke's house today is the Conservative Club. Next to the horse and cart in the old picture (where is the owner?) is the town pump, of which a replica remains today.

The Town Wall, Hartlepool, at the turn of the twentieth century, with Cambridge Buildings on the right and the Fisherman's Arms centre. The Fish Sands below was used as a working environment by the local fishermen, where they moored their cobles (boats) after a day's fishing. It was also used by local people, especially children as a play area, an activity that continues today with everything that entails, such as sand castles, buckets and spades and sandwiches – and there is real sand! The Wall remains today, is Grade 1 listed, and has extensions where Cambridge Buildings once stood and where the old houses were is the Harbour of Refuge (or Pot Inn, as it is also known).

A fine view of the beach at Middleton, looking towards the Town of Hartlepool, with the Pilot's Pier light visible at the extreme right. This Victorian scene shows local children and adults gathered around the fishermen's cobbles, while in the channel are two large fishing vessels making out to sea to the fishing grounds. The steam paddle tug *The Blanche* is also in attendance and clearly visible. An idyllic scene that is much changed today, this beach having been developed for commercial uses, the only recognisable points being the Pilots Pier and the Town Wall.

A gentle stroll along the Town Wall in the early 1900s, a pastime which is still popular today, especially on a fine, warm sunny day. The white building over to the right is that of the Whitby Hotel, while the properties to the left around Sunnyside on the Town Wall are still there, although the middle section, including the hotel, has been replaced with modern housing. The building of the Town Wall probably commenced in 1318 to protect the inhabitants of this prosperous sea-port from attack, mainly by the Scots, and was originally much longer than the present wall.

J.J. Hardy & Sons, Brass Founders of Hartlepool, *c.* 1900, whose foundry stood on the corner of Cemetery Road and Thorpe Street before being transferred to their current Brenda Road site in 1968, where they still produce high grade speciality metal goods mainly in brass and bronze. When the foundry was in full flow at the Hartlepool site they also cast large quantities of high quality bells for churches, public buildings and clocks, as well as instrument cases for the maritime industry.

The Heugh Lighthouse as it appeared around the 1890s; designed and built by Stephen Robinson, it was opened on the 1 October 1847 and is reputed to be one of the first, if not the first, to be illuminated by gas. The original lantern can be seen in the Museum of Hartlepool. After the disastrous naval bombardment in 1914 by German warships the light was dismantled to allow the gun emplacements to cover a wider angle of view, a handicap which prevented some of the returned fire onto the battleships during the bombardment; and the lighthouse was eventually replaced by the present structure complete with fog horn, which is still guiding ships safely into port.

A Christmas card type scene in Middlegate Hartlepool on a winter's day, possibly sometime in the 1930s. The view is from Friendship Lane with the Ship Inn just visible to the left of picture. The building on the right was formally the premises of the Barnett Bros. who in relatively recent times will be remembered by many locals as their regular supplier of tobacco from Mr Barnett's Tobacconists shop. In Victorian times this large building was the offices and works of *The South Durham and Cleveland Mercury*, a local newspaper of note. The tower in the background is of the Hartlepool Borough Buildings, which replaced the original Market Hall in 1929. Much remains on one side of this street, and the Borough Hall is a well-used venue for concerts, exhibitions, stage productions and craft fairs, it being the largest hall in the area.

A view of the ferry at Hartlepool from Middleton to the Town Wall. There were in fact two ferries, the official one and an unofficial ferry operated by local fishermen who charged just a halfpenny each way. In the photograph the main ferry is at the top right while the unofficial one is seen leaving the steps at the centre of the picture. The main usage of the ferries was to transport workmen to and from the Thomas Richardson Engine Works and to William Gray Shipyards during the working week, while at weekends, especially in the summer months, families would flock to the Headland for pleasure visits, especially during

Hartlepool Carnival Week in August each year. The ferry continued to operate into the 1950s.

The Fish Sands, the Town Wall and Sandwell Gate, Hartlepool, from the Pilots Pier around 1895. The fourteenth century Town Wall remains intact today, as does the Sandwellgate, although the square-shaped opening in the wall which was used by the fishermen has been filled in and all the other buildings have long since disappeared. The building to the right of the sandy area is the now demolished Fishermans Arms, and further to the right out of picture was the tenement block of Cambridge Buildings. Prominently in the foreground are the pilots cutters used by Hartlepool pilots to race to an approaching vessel entering the port – first to arrive gets the job of guiding the ship safely into dock.

A parade of The Boy's Brigade Band together with members of The Girls Brigade, marching along the High Street and into St Hilda's church sometime during the 1920s. The High Street buildings in The Croft have all gone, the whole area having been cleared in the 1930s. The High Street exists today, as does a replica of the pump seen in the centre of both photographs. Where The Croft once stood there is now the landscaped Croft Gardens.

WAR MEMORIAL AND LIGHTHOUSE, HARTLEPOOL

Hartlepool's fine War Memorial on the Headland in 1950, with the lighthouse and Cliff Terrace overlooking the scene. The Memorial is dedicated to the men of Hartlepool who were killed during the First World War, and a further dedication was added in 2002 to all those who have died in war up to the present time, including the Second World War. Can it be too much to hope that no further names will ever be added to those already there! In 2002 the grounds were refurbished to a high standard, with new walls and paving together with a new shelter near to the entrance on the seaward side.

Fisher Row on the Headland around the turn of the last century, with the fishermen's cottages complete with pan-tiled roofs and whitewashed frontages, and depicting a fine group of Hartlepool fishwives waiting patiently for their men folk to return with their, hopefully, good catches of fish and crabs - for the livelihood of all their families depended entirely on success at sea. These cottages no longer exist, the whole of this area having been completely redeveloped in recent years.

A romantic view of the High Street, Hartlepool, with St Hilda's church towering above the houses, and in the foreground is the Town Pump behind which are the houses and cottages. The house on the far end of the row to the right is that of Sir Cuthbert Sharp, Baronet, a renowned antiquary, historian, soldier and author of *The History of Hartlepool* published in 1816. Sir Cuthbert mixed in influential circles, being a friend of Sir Walter Scott and Robert Surtees, the Durham county historian, and he was also the Mayor of Hartlepool in 1813, 1816 and again in 1824. He died in 1849.

Chapter 4

PLACES OF WORSHIP

The date is the 8 June 1932, and the occasion is the laying of the foundation stone, and dedication of St Luke's church hall in Welldeck Road, West Hartlepool. The stone was laid by Mrs G.B. Bidgood, wife of the vicar. Many local people turned out for this event as can be seen in the photograph, although the building had a relatively short life, being demolished to make way for housing in the 1970s.

The church of St Hilda can be described as the jewel among Hartlepool churches; the present edifice is made up of many ages, having been greatly restored and added to in 1724, 1863, 1867, 1891 and 1924, although the church was first established on or near to 1190. In 1924 a complete restoration was undertaken of the tower and the chancel. The old picture would be in around the turn of the last century and the church hall can be seen just behind the church on the left. The new entrance porch was completed in 1932. In 1895 the Revd J.F. Hodgson said of St Hilda's, 'For size and sumptuous splendour of decoration, this church is wholly without a rival among the parish churches of its day, not only in the County of Durham, but in the north generally'. The Brus chapel houses the Bruce family tomb, and it is thought that Robert de Brus the forth is buried here, although most of the family were buried at Guisborough Priory church.

Brougham Street, Hartlepool, as it looked at the turn of the twentieth century with, in the distance, the distinctive tower of St Hilda's church. In the centre is St Mary's Roman Catholic church, which was completed in 1851 and is shown complete with elegant spire; next is the Primitive Methodist Chapel, also of 1851 vintage, and which is now demolished. St Hilda's church of course remains today, as does St Mary's Roman Catholic church, minus the spire. St Hilda's church hall was on the left of the picture, and has since been developed and rebuilt into modern sheltered accommodation.

Christ Church in Church Square, West Hartlepool, in around 1900, with a Hansom Cab rank plying for passengers with a group of onlookers, perhaps expecting a local dignitary to appear at any moment. The imposing statue of the founder of West Hartlepool, Ralph Ward Jackson, is prominent in the foreground and today the statue still faces down Church Street where the town started life. The now deconsecrated Christ Church is an art gallery of note, and which also houses the Tourist Information Centre. The church was completed in 1854 using magnesium limestone cut from the dock excavations, the Dock Company providing the materials and the site, and it is interesting to note that the alter rails were made from bog-oak from the sunken forest, excavated from the docks. Ralph Ward Jackson was responsible for this unusually designed town church, although later on there was considerable and serious disagreement between himself and the vicar,, Revd John Burges, sometimes leading to mob violence and disturbances.

A view looking along Victoria Road at around the turn of the twentieth century, with a number of children's groups gathering around or near the open-topped tram. The sight of a large tripod mounted camera would be a draw like a magnet to youngsters in those days, as indeed such an event would be today. The Gray Peverell & Co. Ltd store, complete with dressed windows, compliments the scene, which also includes in the centre the Grand Hotel and the Wesley Chapel. All three buildings remain today, the Wesley now being a leisure centre, nightspot and bar.

All Saints Stranton on Stranton Green, as it was around 1900, which interestingly also shows Stranton Windmill to the left of the church, now part of the J.W. Cameron Brewery; the base of the mill now lies within the brewery storage area. All Saints Stranton is the mother church of West Hartlepool, and dates back to the early fourteenth century, although there is evidence of an earlier church from AD 1129. For over seventy years the church provided the only educational foundation for many miles around, a portion of the building having been bricked off and used as a day school in connection with the Fulthorpe Charity, established in 1707. Contemporary records state, 'In 1865 a handsome turret clock was fixed in the tower of Stranton church by clock maker Robert Hind.' Stranton church continues to serve the community as the parish church of the area.

A scene on Seaton Carew beach during the First World War, showing a group of wounded soldiers sent home from the horrors of the front line to convalescence and recover from their wounds, many of which involved loss of limbs and blindness. Local volunteers including nurses and other ladies who, together with children, formed groups to provide companionship, support and supply cups of tea, as well as organising outings as part of the war effort and to help those in need. Unfortunately many of these veterans were returned to the trenches in France and Belgium, only to be killed or wounded again.

Chapter 5
SEATON CAREW -
VILLAGE BY THE SEA

A view of The Front, Seaton Carew, as it was before the Promenade was built; the sand banks are prominent at the right foreground. Both photographs show the Marine Hotel, and a number of houses and cottages are still standing, although some have been converted to shops. At the extreme right of the old photograph, which probably dates from around 1900, can just be seen the old slip-way which still exists today, and was used by the lifeboat service to launch the horse-drawn lifeboat into the sea whenever their services were required to save lives at sea.

The Promenade at Seaton Carew around the turn of the last century, the tram lines clearly visible at a passing point for trams travelling in opposite directions, there being just one line of track to Seaton. On the foreshore to the left can be seen what is more likely to be a performance by Sunshine Corner, a semi-religious entertainment for children of all ages, with prizes for the young 'volunteer' performers. The lifeboat slip-way is also visible, directly to the fore of the concert area. This view is easily recognisable today and visitors continue to be attracted to the village although it is unlikely to attract the same kind of visitors as in 1812, when the resort was a popular venue for the Quakers of Darlington.

A scene looking towards The Front at Seaton Carew in about 1900, and complete with an open-top tram which plied between the village and West Hartlepool centre. The building on the right designated as a café has long been demolished and was situated at the corner of the Green, where more modern private dwellings have taken their place. And now? - no more trams, just a somewhat lonely milk delivery float, and of course the dreaded yellow lines.

Seaton Low Light on the sea front, not far from where the Staincliffe Hotel now stands, was one of two navigational lights used by mariners to enter Hartlepool and West Hartlepool harbours. This photograph dates from the 1890s and also depicts the row of fine villas, which were built in 1878 and survive gracefully today, an asset to the village. The High Light, the partner to the Low Light, was situated slightly inland and to the north and will be remembered by many people when it was situated on the premises of Batchelor Robinson at Longhill (or Wagga as some would prefer). It has fairly recently been carefully removed and re-erected at Jackson's Landing in the Marina, and dedicated as a fitting memorial to all those who have lost their lives at sea, both in war and peace time.

The Promenade at Seaton Carew in around 1890, and before the sea wall was built. The village of Seaton was developed over a period of time by the Quakers from Darlington as a seaside resort for their families, and they obviously knew a good thing when they saw one. Mr William Tate the Parish Clerk of Stranton, in poetic mood, describes Seaton Carew in 1812 thus: *'By name this devoted Vill/ So adapted that you will/ Your attention bring/ And in support of truth declare/That Seaton and Elysium are/ One and the self-same thing'.*

The Promenade was occupied mainly by houses and cottages and was a gentile place for residents and visitors alike, being a popular 'watering place' for the gentry. The Seaton Hotel at the end of the road is the only public house remaining today from those early days. Some of the early dwellings remain, many converted to shops or amusement arcades, with the Marine Hotel replacing some of the central cottages.

The Green, Seaton Carew in 1910; now three-sided, it originally had four sides, the seaward side falling victim to coastal erosion. The building on the left was the home of Colonel William Thomlinson, a well-known local personality and who was connected with the Seaton Carew Iron Works; prior to which the premises were the King's Head Inn, which was rebuilt in 1803. The building at the end of the road was altered and a new front erected in 1834, although the main structure is thought to be much earlier. Part of the building on the right is now the Norton Hotel and this was formally the George and Dragon Inn, the rest being private dwellings

The Front or Front Street at Seaton Carew in the early 1900s, showing the popular tram system, houses and shops at what was a thriving seaside resort of some significance, founded by Quakers and gradually developed into a popular resort for a family day-out. It remains such today, although it has to said it is in need of some revitalisation and development to cater for the future prosperity of the village. The new photograph depicts on the right the Royal Café and on the left the Seaton Hotel, both of which were there at the time of the early picture, but were just off shot.

Chapter 6

LEISURE TIMES

The very popular and well-known Pierrot Show, which was probably part of the Mascots Concert Party, with its many costume changes during a comprehensive performance on the Hartlepool Lower Promenade Bandstand. The group also performed at similar venues, including Seaton Carew, entertaining visitors and locals during the summer months.

The Hartlepool Headland Open Air sea-water bathing pool in full flow on a fine summers day in 1950. The pool was destroyed during the great storm of 1953, never to be used officially again as a swimming venue. The great storm was one of the worst ever and effected greatly the whole of the East Coast, especially East Anglia, and also Holland on the other side of the North Sea. Apart from a few steps and foundations, nothing remains of the pool or the shelter which in its day proved to be a most popular spot for water sports, swimming and entertainment.

Nestling in the shelter of the Heugh Breakwater and just north of the swimming pool near to the Block Sands, so named because this is where the stone blocks were manufactured when the breakwater was being constructed, is the paddling pool. The pool, mainly due to its very sheltered position, acted like a magnet for families with small children, as the earlier picture, dated 1950, shows. Today the Breakwater is closed to the general public and the paddling pool is in the final stages of refurbishment, so all that is needed now is a little warm sunshine and the youngsters will surely flock back again during the school holidays and at weekends.

Seaton Carew Golf Links, around 1895, and a far cry from the present Seaton Carew Golf Club and its pristine championship standard course. Many championship tournaments have been held on this course and a number of top-class golfers have emerged from this club to join the ranks of national status players. Today the clubhouse is still very recognisable by the twin gable ends, and a number of other building in the vicinity are also still in evidence. During the First World War and again in the Second World War the clubhouse was commandeered by the military and used to house troops usually in transit to the various theatres of war. It is doubtful there would have been much time for golf.

A Nursery school, which in 1946 would be something of a rarity, and mainly reserved for the very young children of mothers engaged in war work. Such nurseries were instigated during the Second World War, to enable women to do the work traditionally carried out by the men-folk, many of whom were away serving with HM Forces. After the war ended, nurseries became a normal part of everyday life and were available to everyone who needed them. The second photograph shows a very informal group on a walkabout from a local nursery on the Headland, and they are obviously enjoying the occasion just as much as they would have done during the 1940s.

Hartlepool Promenade and bandstand area, which was used to stage all kinds of events and which drew great crowds in the process. The turn of the last century photograph indicates one of these events, which is possibly a Pierrot Show, or more likely a Sunshine Corner being very popular with the families. The Promenade was constructed primarily as a sea defence in 1889 but was considerably used for entertainment and spectacle, Empire Day being one of the most popular events, drawing thousands of spectators and participants. In the days long before television, events such as these were the highlights of many people's lives and they took every opportunity to enjoy them.

The Grand Hotel, Swainson Street, West Hartlepool, was opened in 1899 and the picture here would have been taken in around 1910. The building on the left is the schoolhouse of the Wesley Chapel, and the spire St John's Presbyterian church is visible in the distance. The Grand Hotel was built for and owned by the London and North Eastern Railway Company, for the benefit of visitors arriving at West Hartlepool by train at the station, where horse-drawn carriages would pick up passengers for the short journey to the hotel. The Grand Hotel remains to this day although it is now privately owned, and the Wesley is a leisure centre,

nightspot and bar. In the later photograph the building seen on the right is the rear of Hartlepool Civic Centre.

Hartlepool has been endowed with a plethora of musical bands over the years ranging from brass, silver, string, theatre and cinema orchestras, as well as some very fine dance bands. The Picture House Cinema in Stockton Street boasted a fine orchestra led by Mr Angel Bianco, seen here standing with his violin. The film being shown that week was *Slightly Used*, together with *Soft Living*. The cost of the seats in the Front Stalls was 6d, (two and a half pence), the Back Stalls 1/-, (five pence), the Front Circle 1/6d and the Balcony 8d. Large bands today are few and far between, yet Hartlepool hosts one of the finest Big Bands in the United Kingdom, namely the award winning 'Musicians Unlimited', a group of twenty-two extremely talented musicians and singers of high professional standard, led by the talented Mr Mick Donnelly, a musician of national repute and stature. The band is shown performing *The Big Band Sound* during the 2002 Hartlepool Maritime Festival. The vocalist is the 'Frank Sinatra' of the band, (applause please) Mister Bob Caswell, he of the dulcet tones! Another regular singer with the band is Miss Sara 'D', who is noted for her renditions of jazz.

Greenside in Stockton Road, West Hartlepool, in the pre-Second World War period, later becoming the home for children with learning difficulties and then turned into a public house called The Greenside. It was later to be demolished and replaced by a new building and public house also called The Greenside, which has a restaurant and hosts regular quiz nights.

That model of a park, The Ward Jackson, opened in 1883 as a particularly fine example of a Victorian Park, complete with lake, flower beds, trees, elaborate fountain, as well as a number of scenic walkways. Its fine example of a bandstand was presented to the town by Sir William Gray in 1900. The formal terrace garden remains to this day, although the bandstand has been reconstructed together with the ornate fountain. On the extreme right of the old photograph is the bronze statue mounted on a plinth and dedicated to the men of the Boer War, installed in 1905. Sadly during the middle 1960s the statue was stolen overnight, with only the boots left in place, and the plinth remains to this day minus the statue. During the 1930s the terrace flowerbeds were illuminated at night to great effect.

Seaton Carew in the 1930s, being popular with the visitors to the village on day trips to the seaside. Visitors came from the colliery villages to the north and from Stockton on Tees and Middlesbrough to the south, as well as visitors from nearby West Hartlepool. Seaton Carew is now an integral part of Hartlepool and the practice of local visitors arriving by charabanc, train or bus has long since ceased, as there are so many alternative attractions both far and near to attract visitors. However on a fine spring or summer's day and at weekends the resort is still busy, and the fine beach hugely popular for families.

A celebration party for children and adults alike, the occasion being the Silver Jubilee of King George VI and Queen Mary on 5 May 1935. Schools throughout the area were given a days holiday, when street parties were the order of the day and each child was presented with either a medal on a ribbon, an inscribed mug or a commemorative book, depending upon the age group of the child. Today people still celebrate 'al fresco' as the new picture clearly shows, taken at the 2002 Maritime Festival outside the Hartlepool Historic Quay during Her Majesty Queen Elizabeth and His Royal Highness Prince Philip's Golden Jubilee year. Although this particular group consists of adults, the children would not be far away celebrating in suitable fashion.

Lynn Street, West Hartlepool's main shopping street in 1950, probably on a busy Saturday afternoon - and note the complete lack of traffic! On the right is the Hartlepool Chain Library with the Empire Theatre just a few doors along, and opposite can clearly be seen the stores of Marks and Spencers, Boots the chemist, Stanton's Shoes, Freeman, Hardy and Willis, Woolworths, Hardy's Furniture store and, further along, one of the M. Robinson's premises.

Chapter 7
THE DELIGHTS OF SHOPPING

What would have been a familiar scene in Lynn Street, West Hartlepool, in the 1930s; on the right is the Market Building together with the well-known Harry Lamb Clock. Lynn Street was the town's primary shopping street and included most of the national high street names, and many others. About the only building surviving today is the Market Hotel, now an Indian restaurant, and at the bottom end still in existence is the rear and side of The Shades Hotel and the side of the Athenaeum, which both front onto Church Street. New buildings in Lynn Street include Hartlepool Transport Workshops, some council and private offices, and Focus DIY store.

A view of Northgate Hartlepool at the turn of the twentieth century; the Weslyan Chapel on the left was demolished in 1939. Northgate was the premier shopping street on the Headland, and amongst the many shopping names were Page and Company Hatters, the confectioners shop of M. Atkinson, and fruit shop of W. Gibb, then Maynards, famous for their fruit gums. Also in the picture is the Cleveland Arms Hotel, and just off the photograph and to the right stood the Theatre Royal, later renamed The Palladium, and eventually demolished. The buildings have now been replaced mainly by housing, although The Globe Hotel remains as

can be seen in the now photograph, which was taken slightly further back and opposite where the Hartlepool Railway Station once stood in Commercial Street.

Blacketts Department Store in Church Street, West Hartlepool, in the 1950s. Prior to Blacketts, the building was occupied for many years by another departmental store called Hill Carter, and after Blacketts the building was taken over by Dovecot Salerooms. The building survives today and has been restored and turned into a hotel, restaurant on the rooftop and bar under the name of Hill Carter Hotel. The small shop to the left of the store is that of Trotter the Butcher, who ceased trading some years ago.

Middleton Grange Shopping Centre as it was in the 1970s, showing the pedestrian ramp and the central area open to the elements. The original centre was officially opened in 1969 by Her Royal Highness Princess Anne to great acclaim, however the centre was a cold, windy and somewhat soulless place, and typical of the 1960s architecture. The building with the large 'W' on the elevation is of course the Woolworths store. Later the centre was sold by its original owners, Hartlepool Borough Council, to a private developer who completely refurbished the complex providing a much needed roof coverage, escalators, lifts and new flooring, making it what is now a comfortable and bright environment.

Musgrave Street, West Hartlepool, from the Lynn Street end in 1968 just prior to when the first stages of the new shopping centre were due to be completed. Shops here included Ernest Wilson & Son clothiers, Charles Dickens' Tool Shop, Piccadilly Milk Bar, Sparks Confectioners and many others, including The Pram Shop on the opposite side of the road as was M. Robinson's and Walker's the Butchers. Today the whole of this has disappeared completely, even down to the road surface, the area being replaced with a housing development.

Musgrave Street from the Stockton Street end and opposite the Co-op Store, as it appeared in 1968. Shops included in the picture are Bill Nugent House Furnishers and J. Pearlman Soft Furnishings. To the right of the picture and situated on the corner was the Ice Cream Parlour of Mr Di Duca. The space beyond the car is the clearance site of Ward Jackson Primary school, which still exists in name at new premises just around the corner, near to the rear of the fire station. The now picture shows just how much the scene has changed. Musgrave Street has completely gone and has been redeveloped as housing and green open spaces.

The Liverpool House section of M. Robinson & Sons in Lynn Street, which was established in 1875. The photograph was taken in 1966 just prior to the demolition of Lynn Street and the opening of Middleton Grange Shopping Centre, although sadly Robinson's decided not to relocate in Hartlepool, instead concentrating on their other premises in Stockton on Tees and at Leeds. The Liverpool House building is reputed to be one of the first in the United Kingdom to be constructed using the Ferro-concrete system.

West Hartlepool in 1967, a local shopping area near to St Aidan's church and serving the local community. Some of those occupying premises were the Oxford Street Bakery, the Fruit Market, Rule Electrical, Colorossi's Ice Cream, Gardner's Wet Fish, Mrs Pyle's Fish and Chips, the Eclipse Fruit shop, the Co-op Chemists, Handley the Post Office and St Aidan's church hall. As the photograph shows, most of the buildings were empty, boarded up or semi-derelict and awaiting demolition. Opposite was Oxford Street Primary school, later to be transferred to new premises nearby and renamed Stranton Primary school. Housing development has largely taken over this street.

The corner of York Road and Park
Road known as Moorhouse Corner,
well known for carpets, furniture and
furnishings and run at the time by
Mr Ron Richardson, here seen during
demolition in 1976. Next door was the
Audi car showroom of Jock Rae, and
today the site is occupied by Barclays
Bank and a nightspot, the rest of the
land turned over to car parking.

The most prominent building in West Hartlepool is the Central Co-operative Store on the corner of Stockton Street and Park Road, here as it appeared in the mid-1930s. The building was officially declared open in 1915 and is of a very fine classical renaissance design. It occupies the site of an early church school, and the stone is Portland Limestone suspended around a Ferro-concrete framework. This structure has been described as West Hartlepool's finest building and few would disagree. Today the building is a bar, although several attempts have been made to convert it into a hotel and leisure complex, with little success.

At the turn of the last century Lynn Street was a very prosperous shopping street, and this picture shows the Shades Hotel on the left was followed by many shops and a Methodist Chapel, which was used at one time as a venue for boxing training and tournaments. In the 1960s the shops near to the chapel were A. Walker, family butcher, the Beverly Photographic Studio, The Pools Surplus Stores, City Stylish and Hector Grabham, decorators. The old photograph would be from the 1930s.

Douglas R.P. Ferriday. FRSA., AMPA., ABIPP.